Drawing
TIGERS
Using graphite & coloured pencils

First published in Great Britain 2019

Andrew Forkner Natural Art

ISBN: 978-1-67-034493-9

Author's website:

www.andrewforkner.co.uk

Author's Facebook page:

Contents

Dedication:

To all my students, who over the years have inspired me with their interest and enthusiasm.

Drawing

TIGERS

Using graphite & coloured pencil

ANDREW FORKNER

Introduction

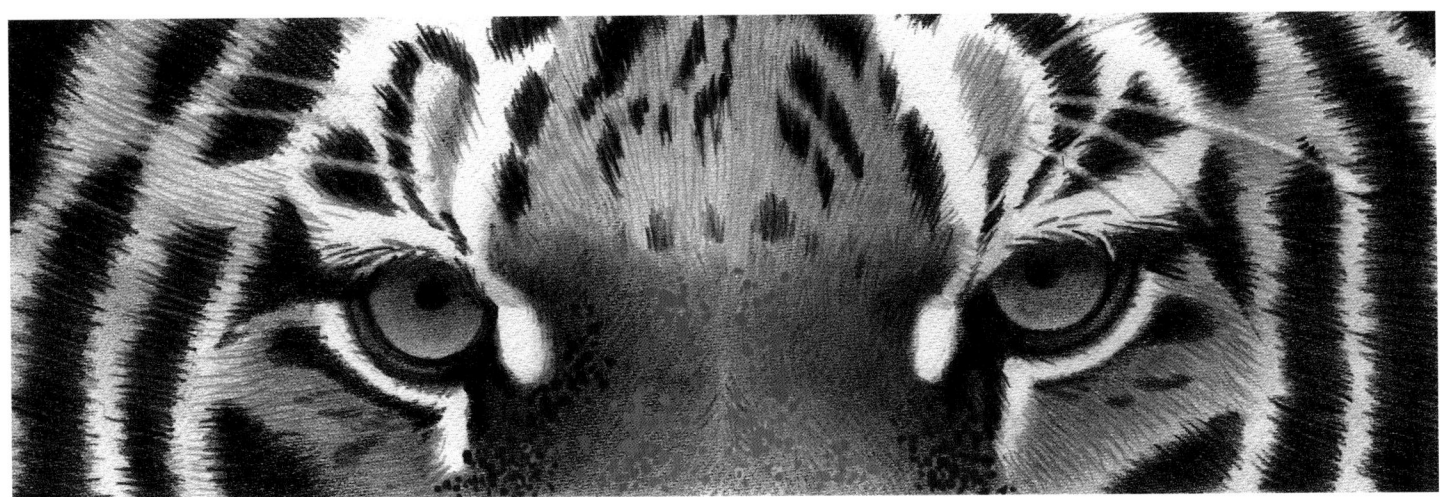

I am constantly amazed and inspired by the wonderful diversity of the natural world. The patterns, colours and textures that can be found throughout nature provide innumerable subjects for artistic consideration.

In this book I will demonstrate the techniques that I use when drawing with graphite and coloured pencils, and I will focus my attention on the tiger, an animal that regularly tops many people's list of their favourite animals.

Coloured pencils, or 'crayons', as we used to refer to them, are a drawing tool that most of us can probably remember from our first colouring attempts at school. The application of colour to a pre-drawn picture can often create striking results, but the presence of the hard, dark outline and the absence of subtle colour changes,   highlights and shadows, prevent it from achieving a truly realistic result.

Working with graphite or coloured pencils is a process that I really enjoy, because of the control that can be more easily achieved than when working with flexible brushes and a wet medium, such as watercolour or acrylic. Modern, 'artist' grade pencils are a pleasure to use, and will repay the extra financial outlay, so always buy the best you can afford.

To help you with your drawing, I have included sections that give details of the different materials and equipment that I prefer to use, along with numerous techniques for creating textures and detail. Other important considerations such as gathering reference information, using sketchbooks, transferring your initial drawing etc. are also covered in detail.

I am assuming at this point that you are reading this book because you are inspired by tigers as a subject for your art, and if I am correct in that assumption then you already have one of the most valuable requirements in order to make your drawing a success. The 'desire' to want to do it is vitally important, because it will help you to cope with times when your drawing doesn't match up to your expectations. You are more likely to return to the composition and have another try, if it is something that you really want to do.

The process of highly detailed pencil drawing can seem daunting, but if you take your time and build the detail and tones in easy stages, then it will be possible to achieve end results that will amaze you.

Be patient and remember the famous quote,

Genius, the power that dazzles human eyes, is often perseverance in disguise.

Materials

Materials
Graphite Pencils

Wood-cased drawing pencils are produced in a range of twenty grades (of graphite/clay mix).

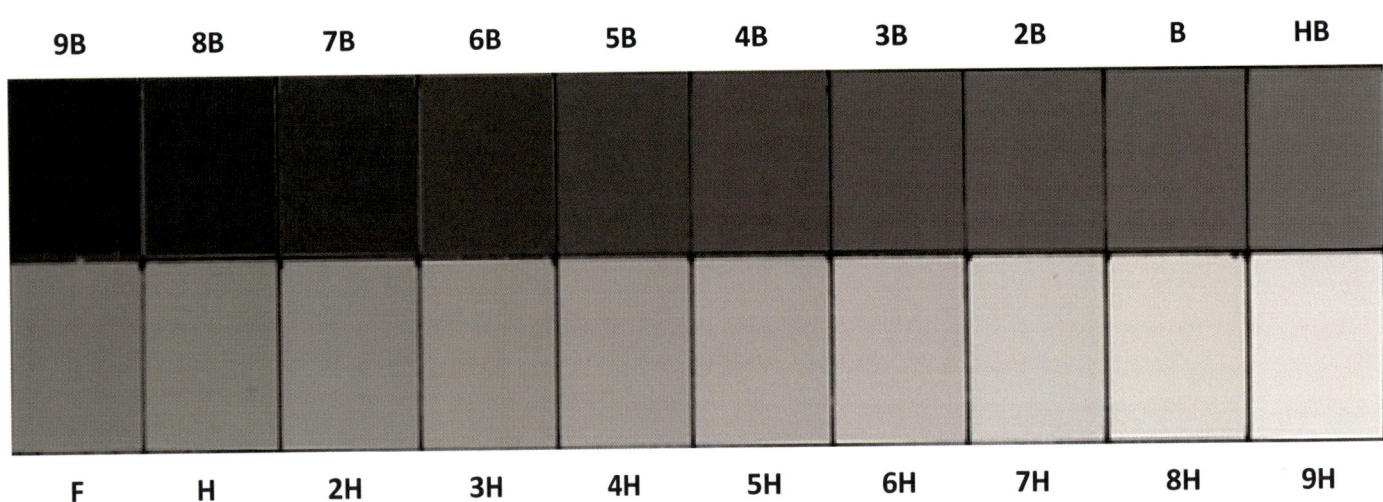

9B	8B	7B	6B	5B	4B	3B	2B	B	HB

F	H	2H	3H	4H	5H	6H	7H	8H	9H

As you would expect, the softest grades deposit the most graphite on the paper, resulting in the darkest lines. It is always advisable to buy good quality art equipment (such as the Caran D'ache Grafwood pencils shown here).

Cheaper pencils are often composed of inferior materials. Wood stems that split, or are not bored accurately to take the graphite, can cause problems when you try to sharpen them. The graphite/clay mix needs to be ground finely to give a smooth, consistent delivery of pigment. Slivers of un-ground clay in the pencil can scratch the surface of the paper and also result in loss of pencil life as you have to constantly re-sharpen them to remove offending sections.

Other wood-cased pencils worth considering.

Derwent: Graphic
Staedtler: Mars Lumograph
Faber Castell: Castell 9000
Koh-i-noor: Toison D'or

Clutch pencils are another way of drawing with graphite. They comprise a 2mm graphite stick (which is also available in a variety of grades) held within the clutch pencil.

My preferred clutch pencils are the Staedtler Mars 780 (shown below). They have a lovely balance to them and are very easy to control. You can sharpen the graphite to a needle sharp point if required, allowing for very detailed drawing. (see lead pointer on page 14)

One advantage of these pencils is that however often you extend and sharpen the graphite (using the lead pointer shown on page 14), the pencil itself retains its length and balance.

Replacement graphite comes in small trays of 12 sticks of the same grade. The tray also contains a coloured tip that can be put into the top end of the pencil (replacing the chrome sharpener) so that you can easily identify the grade of graphite in each clutch pencil.

Water-soluble Graphite Pencils are a wonderful invention! At first glance they appear to be normal pencils, usually in grades, HB (Light wash), 4B (Medium wash) and 8B (Dark wash), like the Derwent Sketching pencil shown here. Once the graphite has been applied to the paper you can dissolve the pigment with water applied with a brush. This gives scope for a further range of textures and can be particularly useful for anatomical features such as eyes (see image below), where you require a dark, clean, sharp edge to the pigment.

Care should of course be taken when introducing water into the drawing process, so moisten your brush and then remove excess water with a tissue before gently touching the brush onto your drawing.

Coloured pencils.

Faber Castell Polychromos pencils are produced in a range of 120 colours and are my preferred pencil.

With an oil-based core they are harder than the more common wax-based alternatives. They hold a sharp, fine point for longer, even on rougher surfaces.

The pencil above has been sharpened with a traditional manual pencil sharpener, giving a shorter, stumpy point.

Prismacolor Premier are a wax-based alternative which are available in a selection of 150 colours.

They are soft textured and offer some different colours that are not available from Polychromos. When working on Pastelmat however they do need sharpening frequently and so I prefer to use them sparingly to add a rich final coat over Polychromos base layers.

This Prismacolor pencil has been sharpened using the Rapesco desk-mounted sharpener (shown on page 14) which produces a longer, finer point, that is ideal for detailed drawing

NB. Prismacolor Premier pencils are sold unsharpened. So care is required to ensure that you sharpen the end opposite the colour name/number, otherwise you will quickly lose that information as you use and repeatedly sharpen the pencil.

Other ranges:

Caran D'Ache Luminance: Excellent quality soft pencils that come in a range of 76 rich colours.

Prismacolor Verithin: Only available in 36 colours, but can be good for fine detailed work.

Derwent Studio: 72 colour range of pencils that are excellent for fine detail.

Derwent Coloursoft: Soft, velvety, rich colours in a range of 72 shades.

Derwent Procolour: These pencils combine the best features of the other two Derwent ranges above.

Choosing your colours

Colour swatches.

For each of my sets of coloured pencils I produce colour swatches (see right).

Taking some strips of drawing paper, I divide each strip into individual sections and using firm pressure I apply each colour to a separate section, along with it's name. The colour runs right to the edge of the strip and this allows the strip to be placed onto your reference photo, (see below), so that you can check which colour is the best match for your use.

11

Paper

Graphite pencil drawing paper. Usually I prefer to work on smooth paper, using Fabriano Artistico Extra White or Bristol Board. If you can afford to buy the thicker (heavyweight) versions of these papers you have the option to indent the surface to create detail. (See techniques/page 20)

Hot pressed Fabriano is smooth but has a slight tooth (texture).

Bristol board is very smooth, allowing for incredibly fine detail.

When working on a drawing that requires me to produce extensive areas of texture and pattern, then I might work on the cold pressed surface version of Artistico, or perhaps Bockingford (See techniques/page 24).

Coloured pencil surface. Coloured pencil drawings can be produced on the surfaces mentioned above, but my favourite is Clairefontaine Pastelmat (see right). This has a coarser surface, but this increased texture means it can accept more layers of colour and paler colours can be applied over darker ones. This paper is also produced in a variety of colours allowing you to choose a complimentary background colour.

Tracing paper. After producing my initial rough drawing on any suitable cartridge paper, I always use tracing paper to transfer the drawing details to the finished surface. (See techniques/page 19).

An alternative to the traditional tracing process is Tracedown, a graphite coated paper that can be placed graphite side down, onto your chosen paper.

Then by laying your outline drawing on top and working over all your lines once again, your graphite outline can be simply transferred to your clean drawing paper.

If you will working on a darker coloured Pastelmat, you can use white Tracedown, to give you a clearer outline. Your coloured pencil layers will gradually cover these white lines as you work.

Other tools and equipment.

1. Camera. I use a Lumix FZ200 'bridge' camera for collecting my reference photos. It has a high spec zoom lens and is lightweight and easily portable.

2. Proportional dividers. These can help you to maintain accurate proportions when enlarging or reducing your drawings. (See page 25).

3. Stumps. These are composed of tightly rolled paper. They can be used to blend graphite lines to 'soften' areas of detail. (See page 22)

4. Koh-I-Noor Hardtmuth eraser pencil. An excellent tool for removing fine lines of graphite from your drawing. Can be sharpened with a craft knife.

5. Tombow Mono Zero eraser. Similar to (**4**), but has a firmer rubber core. Works like a propelling pencil and does not need sharpening.

6. Battery operated eraser. Useful for removing small sections of graphite, especially when used in conjunction with an eraser shield (see right).

8. Large wash brush. This is perfect for removing unwanted debris or graphite dust from your drawing, without smudging.

9. Lead pointer. For sharpening clutch pencils. In use, the tub gradually collects a supply of graphite dust which can be useful for adding extra tone to a drawing using a blender or a watercolour brush.

10. Rapesco desk top pencil sharpener. Creates a nice long point on the pencil.

11. Magnifying glass. Can be useful when working on areas of fine detail, or for checking information in your reference photos.

12. Colour shapers. These rubber-tipped tools are excellent for blending graphite or coloured pencil.

13. Embossing tools. These metal styluses which come in a selection of thicknesses, enable you to purposely indent your paper surface. (See page 20)

14. Pencil extender. Useful when your pencils become too short to hold comfortably.

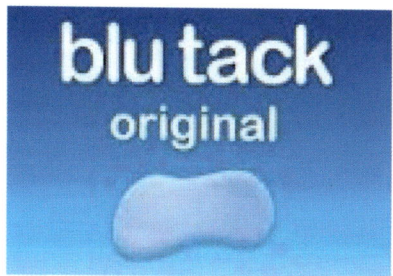

15. Blue Tack (Mounting putty). Great for lifting off graphite to create highlights or remove unwanted marks. It is more malleable than a putty rubber and has better adhesive qualities.

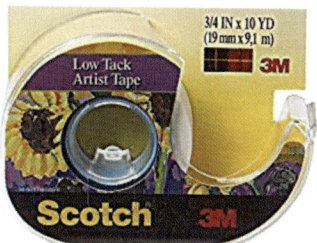

16. Low tack artist tape. Very useful for holding down your drawing, or tracing paper. Can be easily removed without damaging paper surface.

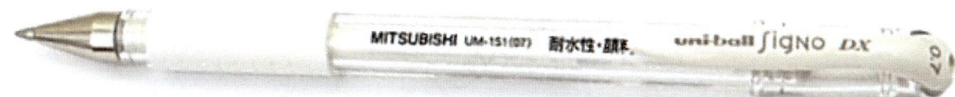

17. White Gel Pen. Can be useful for adding whiskers, or other fine white hair over the top of darker areas of graphite or coloured pencil.

18. Craft knife.

Working space.

Having a designated area in which to work can really help with your development as an artist. A space where your artwork and equipment can be safely left at the end of a session and to which you can easily return to resume work whenever you have time, is a huge benefit.

For many years I made use of the dining room table, which meant that everything had to be moved and stored after each session, eating into the limited and valuable time that I could actually spend on my drawing/painting. Then of course I would have to spend even more time setting everything up the next time I wanted to do any work. This can often create the situation where we actually decide that having to do all of that probably means that there is not enough available time to achieve much and so we decide not to do it at all.

When we do actually begin to work it is also a major advantage to have all our equipment easily accessible and so below you can see a photo of my studio space. It is a small area that is set within a room that also functions as my office.

The smaller the area that you have, the more organised you need to be. I make use of numerous shelves and multi-drawer pencil chests to ensure that everything is within easy reach. Valuable time can also be saved if you know exactly where a particular item of equipment can be found when needed.

Reference material

Photographs

Whenever I am working on a drawing I select a good range of photos of my subject, showing the animal from all angles. This gives me a much clearer understanding of the creature that I am trying to depict.

Taking your own photos. This is a good way of collecting reference images. The photography process forces you to look closely at your subject. With a digital camera it is now possible to gather a vast amount of reference material quickly and easily.

Using photographs from magazines. There is a wealth of high quality photography available in magazines and books nowadays. These can all be used to help you gain a better understand your subject and give you detailed views of specific features.

However*, do not be tempted to copy these images directly as you will be infringing the photographer's copyright.

Purchase reference photos from photographers. Some photographers will happily sell their images, along with either the copyright, or a creative commons licence, so that you can use them in your artwork.

One site that is worth checking out is: **www.wildlifereferencephotos.com**

17

Sketchbooks

Recording details in a sketchbook, in the form of quick sketches, detailed drawings (where the subject will allow), or written field notes, can provide you with a wealth of useful information when you decide at a later date to create a drawing or painting of that particular subject.

As you draw, you are forced to look more closely at your subject than you might otherwise have done and this will strengthen your knowledge of the animal, helping to make your eventual painting/drawing more accurate and successful.

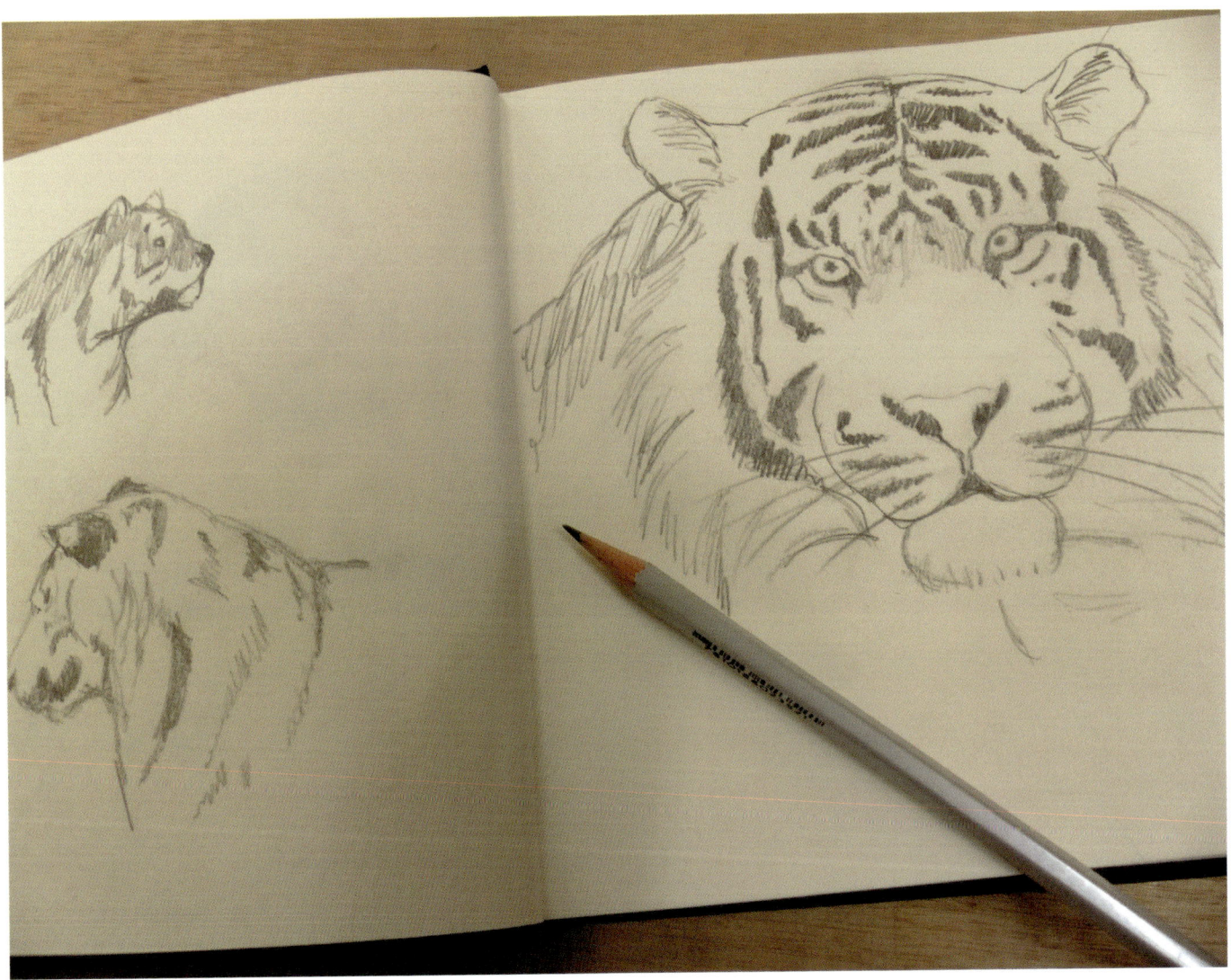

Don't worry too much about the finish of the images that you create in your sketchbook. If your subject changes it's position while you are drawing, then leave that sketch and begin another of it in the new pose. Gradually you will begin to work more quickly and you will find that you are able to record much more useful information in a short period of time, even when your subject is moving around.

The important thing is to draw just what you see. Don't make it up

Sketchbooks come in a variety of formats and sizes, so try a few variations to see which works best for you.

Techniques
Tracing

Stage 1 Lay a sheet of tracing paper over your rough drawing, and using an HB pencil, carefully trace over all the lines.

If the drawing is quite detailed you might find it helpful to put a piece of 'low tack' tape on the top edge to prevent the tracing from moving as you work back and forth across the paper.

Stage 2 Once you have traced all the detail lines, remove your rough drawing and turn your tracing over.

Lay it onto a white surface so that you can clearly see the outline and then re-draw all the lines using a soft (6B or softer) pencil. If you will be transferring the outline onto a coloured surface, use a white pastel pencil (instead of the 6B graphite) for this stage.

Stage 3 Now turn your tracing over once more (so the image is the same way around as your rough drawing), Tape it down onto your watercolour paper (or Pastelmat) and retrace the lines one last time.

Use a hard (4H or harder) pencil, but do not apply too much pressure. Using a really soft pencil in stage 2 means you will be able to transfer your outline, without pressing any indentations into the paper.

Indenting

Stage 1. When you need to indent some detail into your drawing, have your reference photo close by and using your chosen thickness of embossing tool, 'draw' the lines that you want to show up lighter against a dark background.

This is where the thickness of your paper is most important. Thick paper allows you make good, deep indentations, but if your paper is too thin, you are more likely to accidentally push graphite into the shallower grooves in the next stage, resulting in less distinct, pale lines.

Stage 2. Take a used stump (already impregnated with graphite) and gently work across the indented lines. The graphite will begin to tone the paper surface, but will leave the Indentations clean. If you need to darken the area even more, then you apply more graphite to the stump by rubbing it on a 9B pencil and then work over the drawing again.

Repeat this process several times and this will create lines of varying tone to give more depth to the detail.

For some detail areas that require indenting, such as whiskers, your indented lines will need to be drawn quickly and smoothly to give a realistic result.
Take another small piece of the paper that you are drawing on and practice getting the clean sweeping lines that you are looking for.
This a process that needs to be right first time, so don't commit to indenting your actual drawing until you are confident in your technique.

Pencil techniques.

When applying graphite, if you are trying to create an even tone in your drawing, take a bit of time to practice the technique shown in photo 1 (see right).

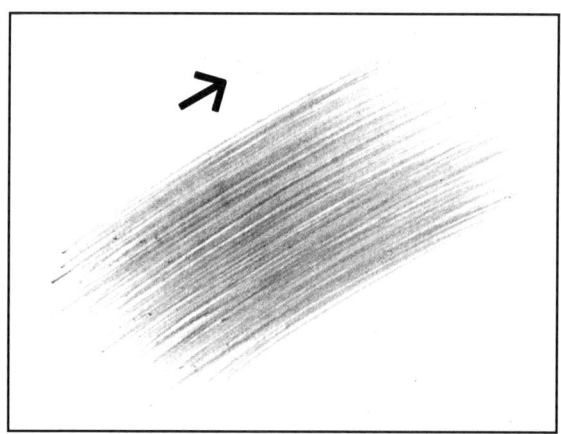

In this exercise I have drawn a series of lines, moving my pencil in one direction only across the paper. At the end of each stroke I lift the pencil and repeat the (left to right) stroke . The result of this gentle 'stroking' technique is to create a more even tone and a soft, feathered edge to the tonal area, which can be more easily extended across the paper, without the creation of any distracting darker areas where lines overlap.

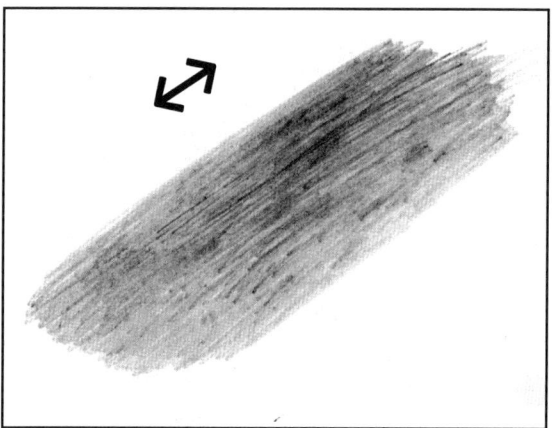

Using the more familiar 'back & forth' method, (see right) where you do not lift your pencil from the paper surface, you tend to create harder, unnatural, linear edges to the tonal area and also a greater variation of tone within your shading.

If you need to create natural texture in your drawing, perhaps in background elements of your picture (eg. For rocks, or tree bark) then using a rhythmic, continuous, circular application of graphite, can help to produce a suitable textural pattern.

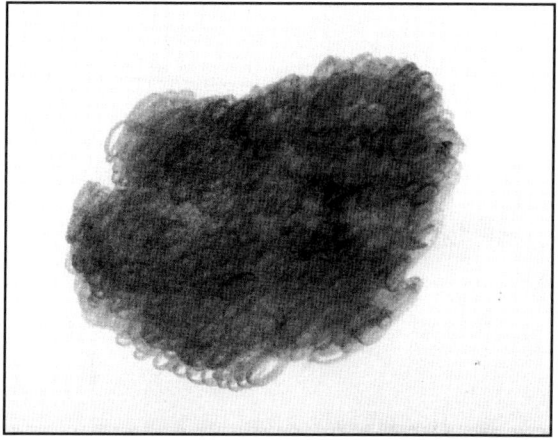

In the picture to the right I have used a blunt, 6B pencil and randomly worked around on the paper, gradually building up a varied pattern. You can see the circular pencil lines more clearly along the bottom of the dark shape.

In this final picture I have worked over the previous image with mounting putty, shaped into a point.

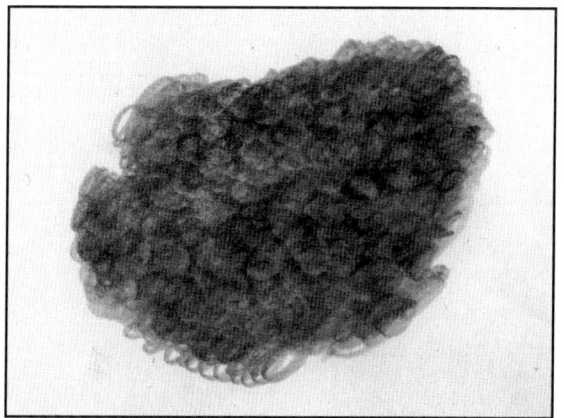

By dabbing the dark graphite repeatedly, I have removed small sections of darker tone and created an even more varied texture. The use of mounting putty can often achieve some interesting effects. Successful drawing can often result as much from what you take away, as what you add.

Using a blender to create a smooth, even tone.

Apply graphite to the paper using fairly even pressure to create a succession of parallel lines.

Although lines like this can often be used to indicate a particular pattern, or texture, there may also be times when you require a more even finish to the application. This is where you can employ your blenders to merge the lines together.

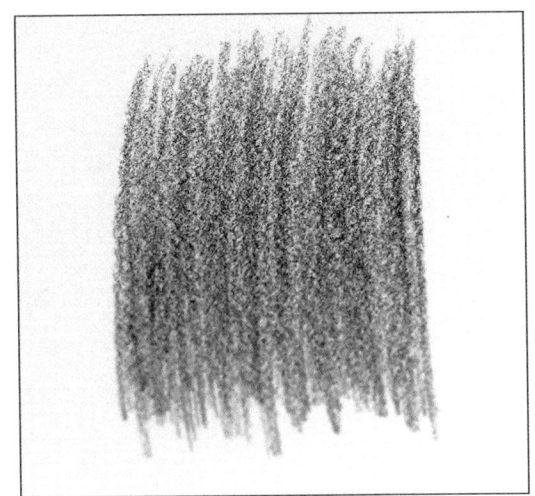

Using a paper (stump) blender work back and forth (in all directions) across the graphite area and gradually merged the lines into a more even covering on the paper surface.

Lifting out graphite to create detail or highlights.

In this image you can see that I am removing some of the graphite layer using my Blu Tack (mounting putty). By keeping the Blu Tack warm in my left hand while I draw, I can then use it to lighten areas that may be too dark, or to create highlights. It can be squeezed to a suitable shape and repeatedly touched gently against the paper surface to remove some graphite.

For comparison the sharp, pale line to the left in this photo was made using the Hardtmuth eraser pencil.

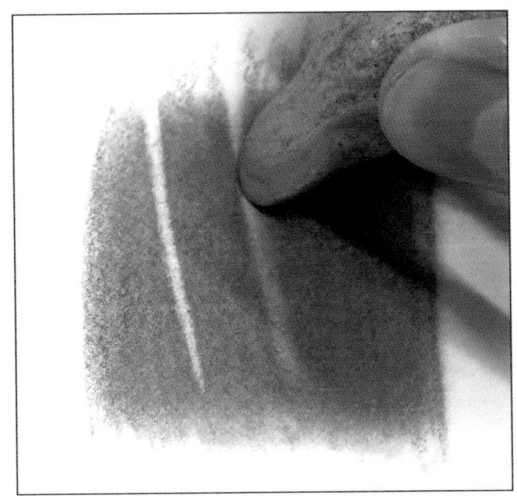

As indicated in the 'Indenting' section, once you have used a blender and it has become impregnated with graphite, you can then use it to add tone to other areas of your drawing. The shape of these applied areas can be easily adjusted using your Blu Tack.

NB When using Blu Tack to remove graphite, make sure that you do not scrub it across your drawing as you would with an ordinary eraser. Just squeeze it to shape and gently touch it against the graphite and lift it away. Repeat this process until you reach the desired level of tone.

Pencil pressure

By varying the pressure that you apply when using pencils, you can achieve subtle variations in the resulting tone/colour that you create. The harder that you press, the less the fibres and textures of your surface show through your colour application.

There are of course infinite degrees of pressure that can be used, but for the sake of simplicity in the step-by-step demos I will just refer to light, medium and heavy pressure.

Light pressure:

Holding the pencil further away from the tip than normal and making sure than the pencil point is rounded (not sharp) helps you to apply a light layer of colour.

This can be useful for subtle colour changes within a drawing, or for delicate areas of shadow, where you still require some of the previous layer of colour/detail to show through.

Medium pressure:

Using the pencil as you would if you were writing with it, will give you a medium tone.

This is the degree of pressure that I use for most of a drawing. You can always increase this tone by applying more colour on top, or lighten if needed using the mounting putty.

Heavy pressure:

By pressing really hard you can flatten the surface texture of your paper and get a rich, deep tone.

In the top left corner of each of these samples, you can see where I began with a very sharp point to each pencil. The sharper the point, the darker your resulting colour will be and the less surface texture will show through.

Creating texture detail using cold pressed watercolour paper.

When you need to create rough textures using graphite pencil, one way of speeding up that process is to choose a coarser surface to work on.

Using an impregnated blender on cold pressed watercolour paper, such as Fabiano Artistico, allows you to take advantage of the paper's inherent texture.

As you work back and forth over the surface, your blender will leave graphite on the ridges, but leave the Indentations cleaner in a similar way to the technique on page 20.

NB: The texture pattern on some manufacturers (cold pressed) paper, is very uniform and not particularly natural in appearance, so try a few different types to find one that suits your needs. Many suppliers will sell small packs of sample sheets, so that you can try a number without a huge financial outlay.

One further consideration when choosing a cold pressed paper, is whether you can still create the level of detail that you require in your drawing. A paper that is too textured may inhibit your potential to achieve that.

Below you can see the resulting texture that I have achieved by applying graphite with a blender onto :

Bristol Board (sample A)

Bockingford watercolour paper (sample B)

A	B

 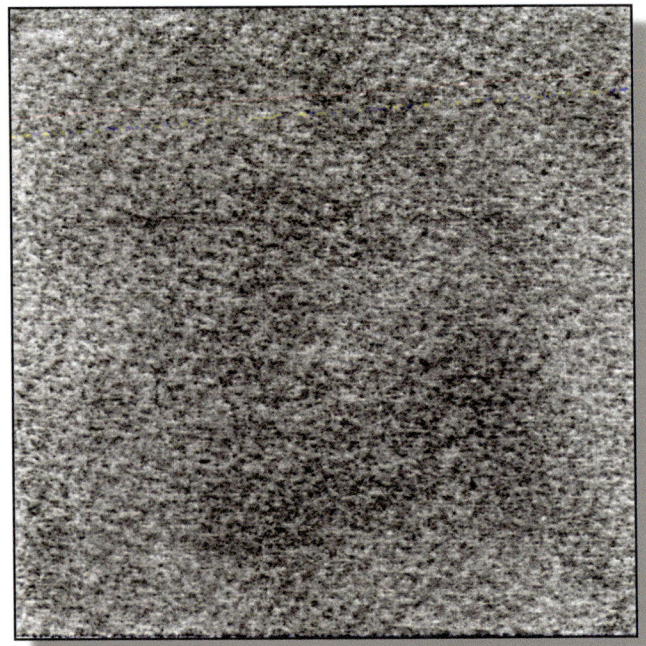

Starting your drawing.

If you are confident in your drawing ability and work freehand directly from your reference image, you can use scale (proportional) dividers to check that you are maintaining the correct proportions.

If you are changing the scale of the image, the central pivot on these dividers can be moved along a calibrated scale and positioned against the value of your desired enlargement/reduction.

In the photo the pivot is set at a value of 2. So when I place the two small points on a specific section of the drawing (such as the distance between the ears), then the two larger points at the other end of the dividers will be automatically twice as far apart. This larger dimension can then be applied to my new drawing to check that I am getting the proportions correct.

Conversely, if I place the two larger points against the same section of the drawing, then the distance between the two small points will be half of the original, enabling you to create an accurate reduction.

There are numerous versions of these dividers available from art equipment suppliers at very reasonable prices.

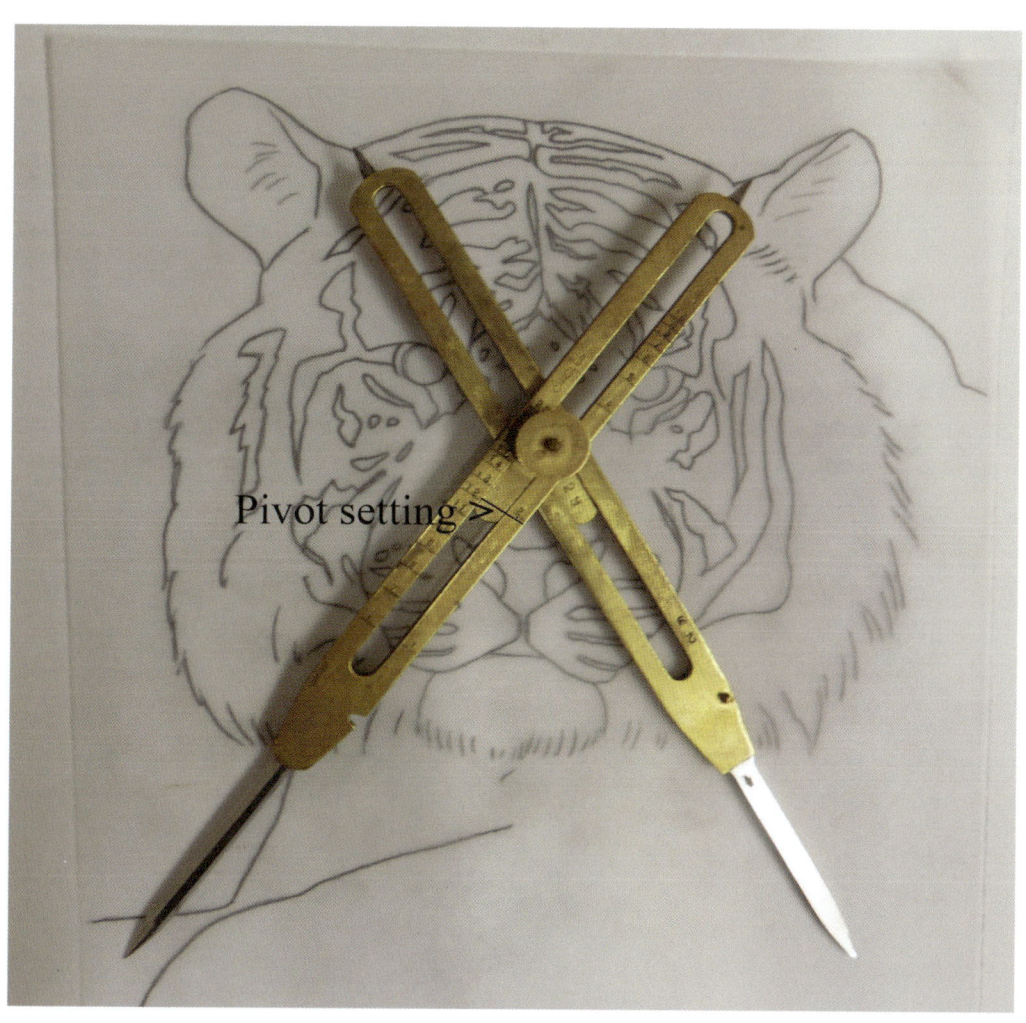

Pivot setting >

Grid method.

This method makes the process of drawing much simpler, by allowing you to focus on a small section of the reference image at a time. This helps to ensure that the proportions and position of features are correct.

Firstly, in a word processing programme, such as Microsoft Word, create several grids (tables), each with square pattern of a set size. I would most often use either a 2.5cm, 2cm or 1.5cm square size but you can make your grids any size that best suits your needs.

Then print (on clear, A4 overhead projector acetate film) one copy of each grid size. This will allow you to work from reference photos of any size up to A4.

In the image below you can see my reference photo with the 2cm transparent grid laid over the top.

Next, to create a drawing:

Print the desired size grid onto plain white paper and begin to systematically copy the detail from each small square of your reference photo into the corresponding square in your 7 x 6 paper grid (see below).

To make your drawing the size of the original, choose and print the same 2cm grid onto your paper.

Alternatively, you can enlarge it by printing out and drawing onto a 2.5cm (or a larger size) square grid, or reduce it by choosing the 1.5cm (or smaller) grid.

For greater enlargements, if you only have an A4 printer and 7 x 6 squares of your chosen size will not fit onto an A4 sheet, you can print several sheets and tape them together to give you the bigger 7 x 6 grid.

When you have completed as much of the detail from your reference as you require, you can trace the outline (see: Techniques page 19) or use Tracedown (see page 12) and transfer this image to your chosen surface to begin building the detail.

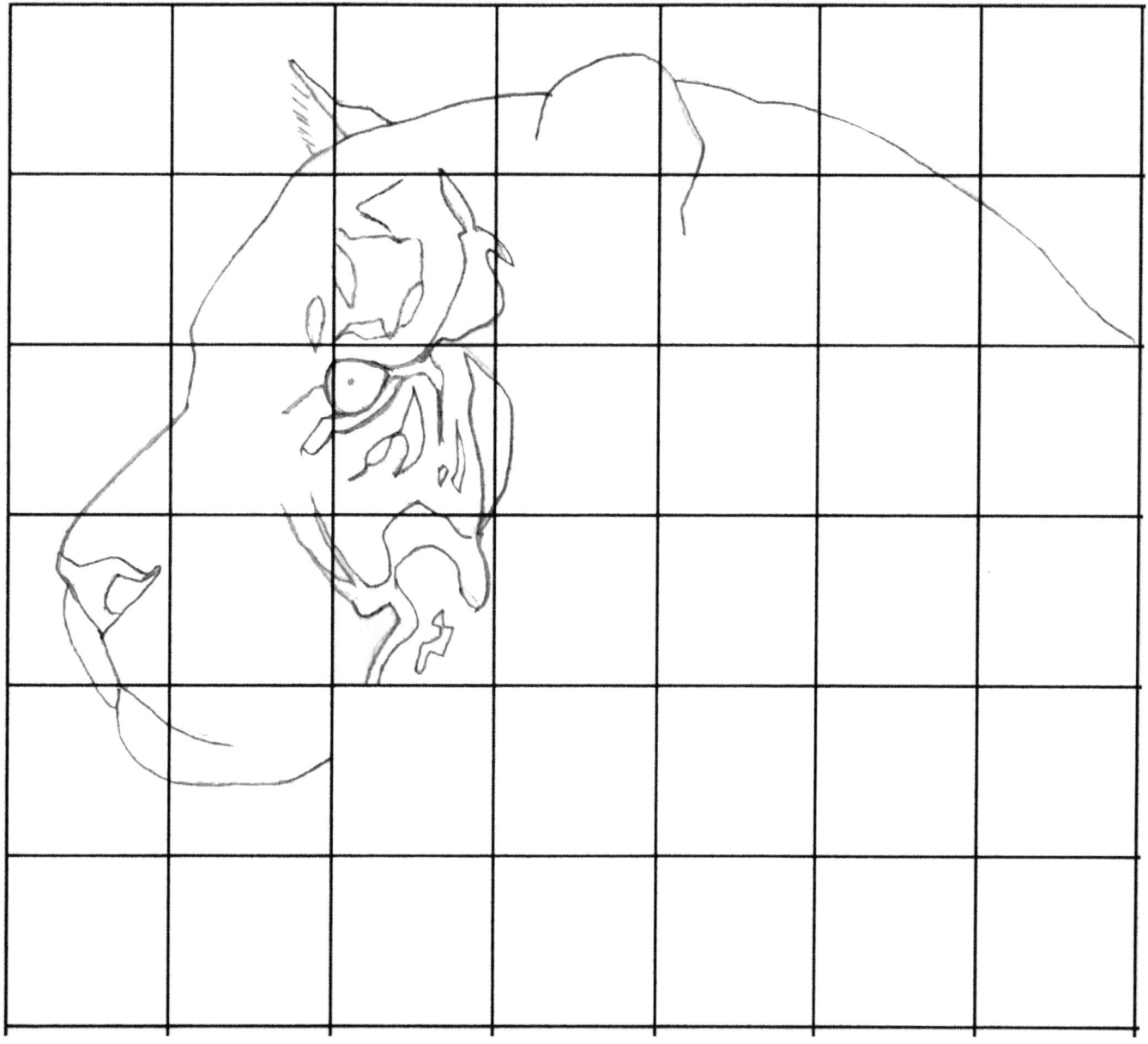

Features

Fur

When drawing any (hairy) animal it is important to understand the direction in which the fur grows on the creature's body, especially on the head and face.

In the diagram below you can see how the fur radiates out from around the eyes and over the rest of the head. The fur on the nose and muzzle is very short and almost suede-like. Elsewhere on the head it becomes gradually longer, the further it is situated from the eyes.

Getting these growth directions right is especially important along the irregular edges of the black stripes, where these fine dark hairs can help to indicate the shape and form of the head.

Eyes

Unlike the eyes of the domestic cat, which have a vertical slit shaped pupil (see right), those of all the big cats have a round pupil.

When drawing the eyes, it is important to try to obtain really clear, detailed reference photos, so that you can include the wonderful colour variations and patterns that can be found in the iris' of these animals.

Creating effective shadows and highlights on the eye surface is also

crucial to giving the impression that it is curved and moist. Highlights should be graduated from bright white to pale grey/blue. This helps to show that one point of the eye is directly facing the source of illumination, but as the surface curves away it receives a little less light. Shadows should also be drawn to show this curvature and illustrate the fact that the eye sits back behind the eye lids.

The two images shown here are drawn with coloured pencil on Clairefontaine Pastelmat paper.

Drawing
TIGERS

Step by step drawings.

On the following pages you will find some demonstrations (in both coloured pencil and graphite pencil), of how I draw some of the important features of Tigers, followed by two detailed 14-stage portrait demos.

For each demonstration I have given details of the paper and pencils that I have used, but it is important to say at this point that these are my personal choices and not 'hard & fast' examples that must be used. I would encourage you to try various alternatives, to find the ones that work best for you.

Where I have chosen a particular brand of pencil that you might not ordinarily use, then see if you can match the colour within your preferred range, rather than investing in more new pencils.

However, if you are tempted to experiment, then there are currently many ranges of 'artist' quality pencils available (see page 10), each with their own particular colour range and texture.

Tiger fur in coloured pencil.
Paper: Dark Grey Pastelmat. **Derwent Lightfast Pencils:** Black, White, Sandstone, Apricot, Dark Orange, Cloud Grey

Reference photo.

1. I have begun by adding the base detail layer of the **White** fur, using medium pressure and varying the length of the of the pencil strokes, to show the variation in the fur.

2. Using my **Black** pencil and the same process as in the previous stage, I have introduced the first layer on the stripes.

3. This is a simple stage, where I have applied the first layer of **Sandstone** colour, using medium pressure.

4. Having applied an additional layer of each colour, using heavy pressure, I have now begun to create the textural shapes within the fur.

5. In this final stage I have added shadows within the White fur using **Cloud Grey** with light pressure. I have tightened the detail of the **White** and **Black** fur, using heavy pressure and a very sharp pencil. On the orange fur I have applied layers of short (light pressure) strokes of **White** then **Apricot** to create texture. Finally, I have added shadows using **Dark Orange**.

Tiger fur in graphite pencil. Paper: Bristol Board 250gsm.

Caran d'ache Grafwood pencils: 2H, B, 4B, 9B. Stump. Koh-i-noor Hardtmuth eraser.

Reference photo

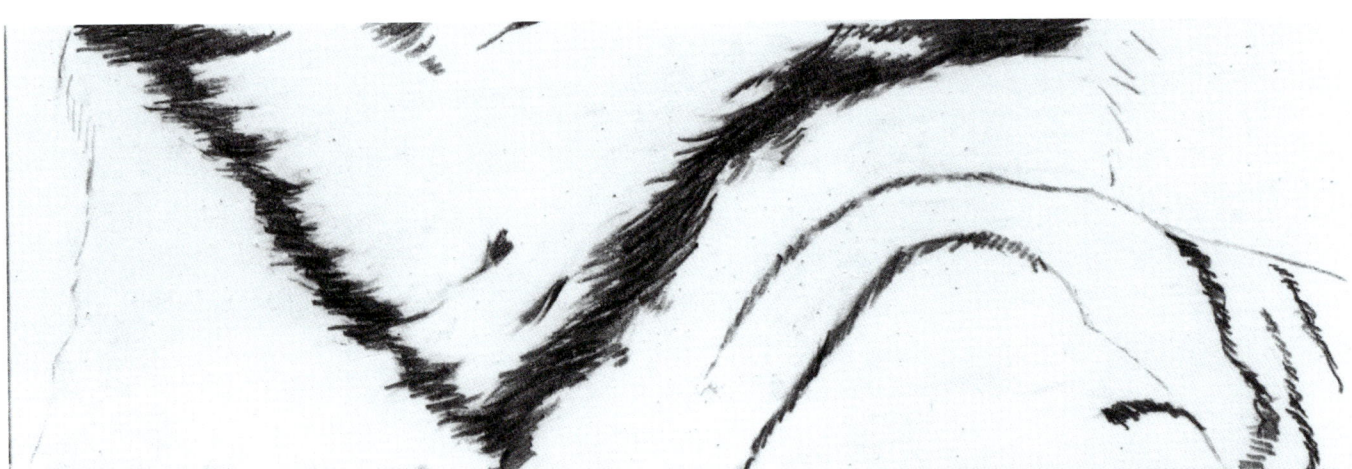

1. I started by roughly establishing the black stripes using the **4B** pencil (medium pressure). All the pencil lines following the direction of the fur growth.

2. Using the **2H** pencil (light pressure) over the white fur area I put in the soft shadows, which help to create the shape of the tufts of fur.

34

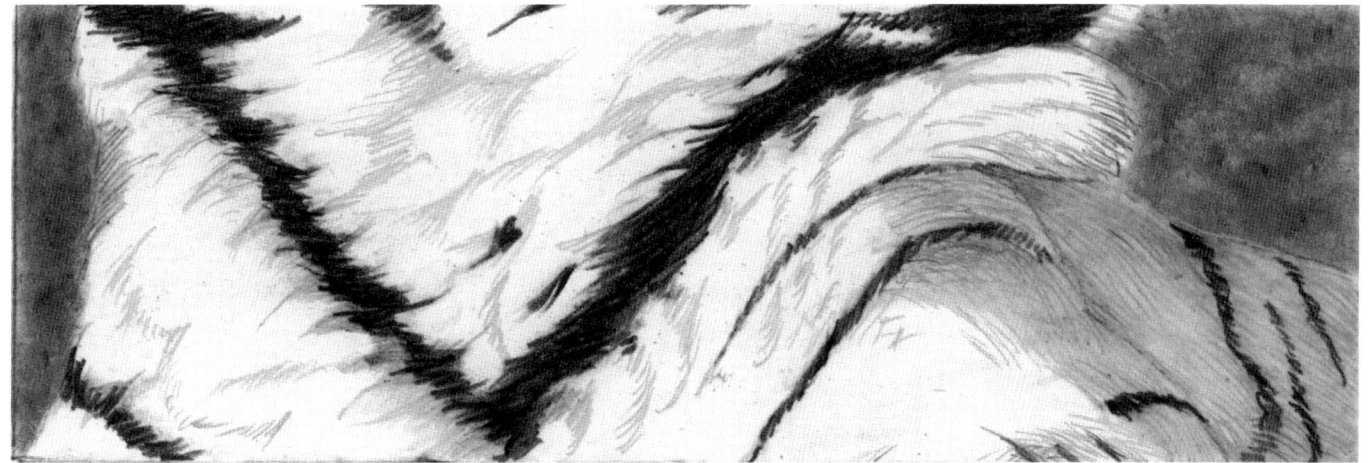

3.In this third stage I have used the **stump** to create a dark background. Then with the same stump I added a base layer to the orange fur. Over this base I then used the **B** pencil to add short detail lines and some shadows to this fur area.

4. After adding more tone to the background, I have created the fine fur edges using the **Hardtmuth eraser** to 'draw' the fur. I have also removed some fine, pale detail lines over the back and shoulder with the **eraser.**

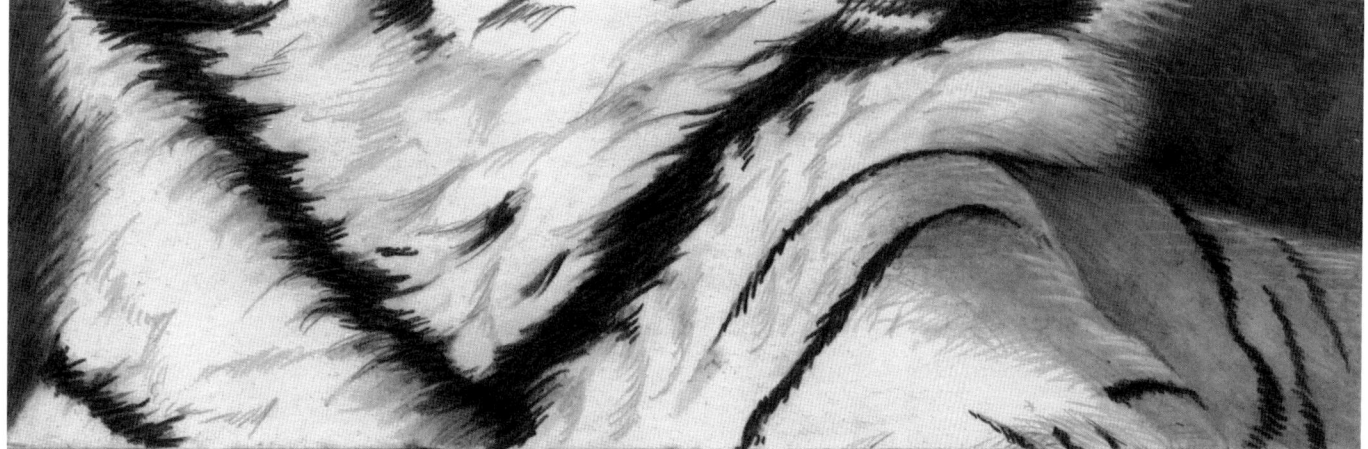

5. This final stage is all about refining the detail. With a sharp **9B** pencil (heavy pressure) I have worked over the black stripes. To finish I used the **B** pencil to increase the shadows on the throat fur and also over the shoulder.

Tiger's eye in coloured pencil.
Paper: Pastelmat dark grey. Derwent Lightfast Pencils: Black, White, Sandstone, Apricot, Dark Orange, Cloud Grey, Champagne, Mid Ultramarine.

Reference photo.

1. Using my **Black** pencil with medium pressure, I established the stripes, eye ring and pupil.

2. Using the **Sandstone** and **White** (both medium pressure), I have blocked in the other fur areas. On the eye I have applied **Champagne** to the iris, leaving a small area for the highlight.

3. For this stage I applied **Cloud Grey** over the iris, leaving a curved section of the pale yellow colour showing along the front edge. I have added the White highlight and reduced it's intensity over the pupil by adding a small patch of **Mid Ultramarine.** To the top of the eye I have created a shadow with **Black** (light pressure). I have added more **Black** (heavy pressure) to the pupil and the skin around the eye.

4. Continuing to increase the tone I have applied **Black, White** and **Apricot** to their respective fur areas, using heavy pressure. Then using the **White** pencil (light pressure) I have added some pale detail lines over the orange fur.

5. To finish I have used sharp **Black** and **White** pencils to add more detail to the stripes and then applied **Mid Ultramarine** to the highlights on the skin around the eye.

Tiger's eye in graphite pencil.

Paper: Bristol Board 250gsm.
Caran d'ache Grafwood pencils: 2H, B, 4B, 9B. Stump. Koh-i-noor Hardtmuth eraser.

Reference photo.

1. To begin I have roughly established the dark detail with the **4B** pencil (medium pressure) making sure to leave the highlight area of the eye.

2. On the iris I have created the 'colour' by applying tone with the **2H** pencil leaving a pale section on the front edge of the eye.
With the **9B** pencil (heavy pressure) I have also darkened the pupil and eye ring.

3. On the top edge of the eye I have applied a shadow with the **4B** pencil (light pressure).
Using the **Stump** I have extended the dark area in front of the eye.

4. Where the fur is orange I have applied graphite using the **Stump** to create a base layer and then added fine detail lines using the **B** pencil.

On the dark section in the lower right I have added detail with the 4B pencil.

5. Most of the refinements applied to this final section are applied with a sharp **9B** pencil (heavy pressure) to create finer detail along the edges of the dark stripes.

A few lines are added to the white fur using the **2H** pencil.

Tiger's ear in coloured pencils.

Paper: Dark Grey Pastelmat. Derwent Lightfast Pencils: Black, White, Sandstone, Apricot, Dark Orange, Cloud Grey

Reference photo.

1. Using my **Black** pencil I have established the dark areas of the drawing.

2. I have now applied a layer of **Sandstone** to the 'orange' fur areas.

3. With the **White** pencil I have now added some detail lines over the **Sandstone** base layer and also begun to define the complex fur within the ear.

4. In this stage I first drew in the wispy hairs using medium pressure and my **White** pencil.

Then I carefully applied more **Black** to the ear recess, using a sharp pencil and heavy pressure, taking care not to overlap the white hair detail.

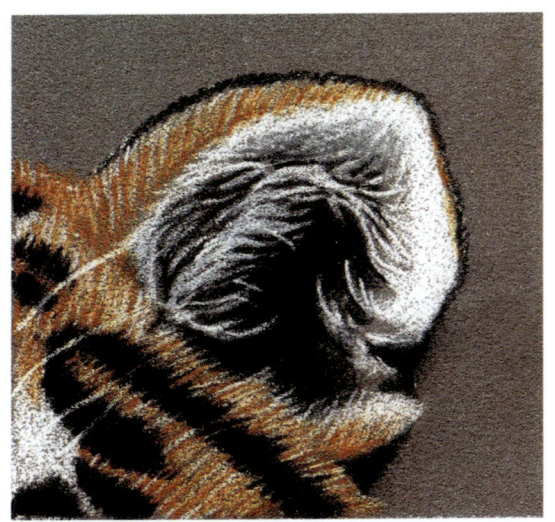

5. To finish this drawing I have added more **white** hairs in the ear using a sharp pencil (heavy pressure).

I used the same pencil to add the fine whiskers.

Finally I have also applied a light pressure layer of **Apricot** over the orange fur to create a richer colour and more **Black** over the stripes to define them more clearly.

Tiger's ear in graphite pencil. Paper: Bristol Board 250gsm.

Caran d'ache Grafwood pencils: 2H, B, 4B, 9B. Stump. Koh-i-noor Hardtmuth eraser.

Reference photo.

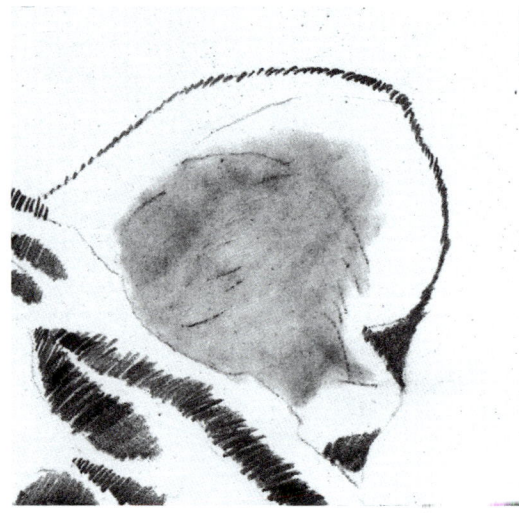

1. To begin I have drawn in the Black areas using the **4B** pencil (medium pressure).

I have also introduced the mid-tone of the ear recess by rubbing some graphite onto the paper with my Stump.

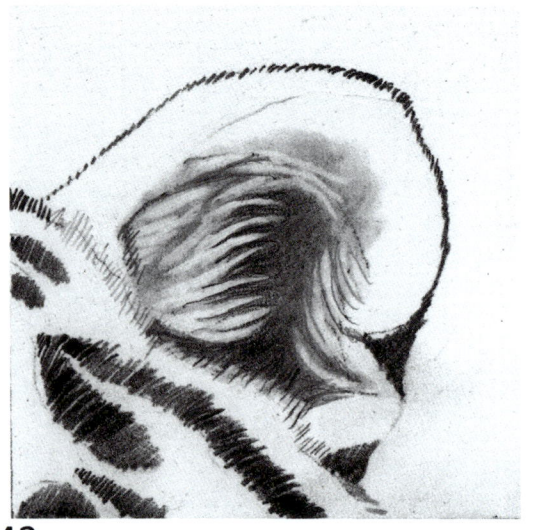

2. Using the 'sharpened' **Hardtmuth eraser** I have now begun to establish the hair detail within the ear, by erasing fine lines across the mid-tone area.

With a sharp **4B** pencil I have added more dark tone to the mid-tone area to emphasise the recess.

42

3. Here I have applied more tone to the edge of the ear and to the wispy hair using the **Stump** once again.

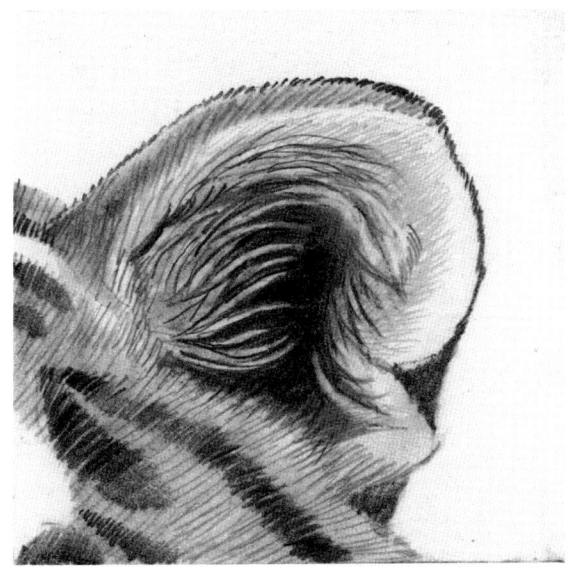

4. Now I have added the remaining 'orange' fur areas, by applying more graphite with the **stump**, before drawing in some fine detail lines over the top of this layer with the **B** pencil.

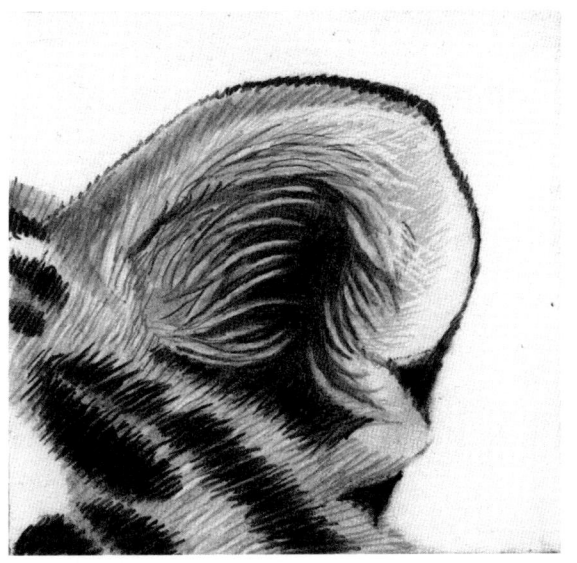

5. To complete this final stage I have added more tone to the ear and the stripes, using a sharp **9B** pencil .

Tigers
Siberian Tiger (Panthera tigris tigris)

Cat stats

Height (at shoulders): 110 cm

Head/body length: 2.4—3.7 m

Tail length: 60—90cm

Body mass (average): Male 178Kg Female 118Kg

The Siberian (sometimes known as the Amur) tiger frequents the cold regions of far eastern Russia and north east China.

All sub species of tiger are very similar in appearance, but some variations occur in body size and coat colour/length.

Even within species there can be a marked variation with the Siberian sometimes paler in colour. The black stripes that are the distinctive feature of all tigers can be a very dark brown in these paler animals.

Step by step portrait using coloured pencils.

Materials: (See Materials section pages 8—15)

Surface: Clairefontaine Pastelmat board (Dark Grey)

Coloured pencils:

<u>Polychromos (**PC**)</u>: Black, White, Terracotta, Green gold, Cream, Medium Flesh, Cold Grey IV,   Warm Grey IV, Warm Grey V

<u>Derwent Lightfast (**LF**)</u>: Sandstone, Apricot, Dark Orange, Mars Orange, Venetian Red, Vandyke Brown

Graphite pencils: HB (also 6B & 4H If you are tracing the drawing)

Other papers: Cartridge paper (if you using the grid method), White Tracedown or Tracing paper, depending on your preferred transfer method.

Mounting putty.

For this drawing I have chosen to work on the dark grey Pastelmat mentioned above, because in the areas of white fur on the tiger the grey paper will show through the white pencil strokes in places and help to give the impression of shadow lines within that fur.

Using a coloured surface means that if you prefer the Tracedown method to transfer your drawing you will need to use the 'white' version to ensure that you can clearly see your resulting outline.

Scan this code to watch a timelapse video of the complete drawing.

To begin this drawing you can either trace the outline shown above, or create your own outline using the grid method shown on pages 24 & 25. If you use the grid method and you want to increase the size, don't forget to create your second grid with larger squares. If you have traced the image directly you can place this into a photocopier to create a larger version. Once you have prepared your outline you are ready to transfer it.

Here you can see the result of having transferred my outline drawing using the White Tracedown. (See page 12) Using tracing paper (with white pastel on the reverse. See page 19) would result in the same white outline. As you work through the drawing process you can gradually cover, or remove the white outlines.

Using my **Black** and **White** pencils (medium pressure), I have applied a layer of coloured pencil to the relevant areas of the tiger. I have made sure that my pencil lines are applied in the direction that the fur grows (see page 26).

The length of these applied lines are dictated by the length of fur the I am depicting.

Using the **Sandstone** pencil (medium pressure), I have proceeded to add the first layer to the 'orange' fur areas. In these initial stages I am effectively just 'blocking in', without being too concerned with specific detail. Once again the colour application follows the direction of fur growth, but there is still   plenty of the grey paper showing through

Now I have begun to add more detail.

Using heavy pressure I have added a layer of **Cream** over the area of the eye, then applied **Cold Grey IV** over that, making sure to leave a narrow line of **Cream** showing along the lower edge of the eye.

Once again, using heavy pressure I have increased the tone of the **Black** border around the eye, creating an irregular line along the top edge, to indicate where some of the **White** fur overlays the **Black**. I have also reinforced the pupil with another layer of **Black**.

Next I have applied a light pressure layer of **Black** over the top section of the eye to create a shadow and using heavy pressure I have created the curved highlight with the **White** pencil.

Moving on to the facial fur I have applied (medium pressure) **White** pencil over the orange fur , leaving some of that layer showing through. I have also used my 'sharp' **Black** pencil (heavy pressure) to begin to create detail along the edges of the black stripes.

Gradually moving away from the eye, I have added more detail with short strokes and a combination of sharp **White** and **Apricot** pencils, using a medium pressure.

Just to the left of the eye I have added a shadow, using light pressure and my **Cold Grey IV** pencil.

Using heavy pressure and my **Black** pencil I have darkened the black stripes on the forehead and covered some of the white outlines that were visible in the previous image.

When working on detailed areas of the drawing on Pastelmat paper or board, you will find that the textured surface will blunt your pencil's point quite quickly. It is important to be prepared to re-sharpen your pencils regularly.

There will be times when a soft, indistinct finish is required, such as when applying delicate shadows, but for detail a sharp pencil is essential. The sharp point will also create a more 'saturated' colour, as the point pushes more pigment into the texture of the paper and obscures the underlying paper colour.

Continuing to focus on the same area I have overlayed the previous layers with another (light pressure) application of **Apricot**. The pale lines of detail created in the previous stage are still visible, but have been 'softened' so they are not quite so obvious.

Along the cheek section I have applied **Apricot** and **White** as before, whilst in the 'tear' section just in front of the eye I have begun to darken the fur using **Vandyke Brown** (light pressure) .

The black and white areas on the cheek have been reinforced using sharp pencils and a heavy pressure application.

Where I have begun to extend the 'orange' fur colour down the muzzle, I have covered the previously visible white outline.

Continuing to use the **Apricot** and **Vandyke Brown** pencils I have completed the (light pressure) application down the length of the muzzle to the nose.

The fur in this area is very short and suede-like, so I have allowed the texture of the Pastelmat to create the impression of the fur.

In this section the benefits of a light pressure application can be clearly seen. Where I have applied the **Vandyke Brown** in front of the eye, it is still possible to see the base colour showing through the subsequent darker layer. This gives the drawing a much more subtle, 'realistic' finish.

If you find at any stage that you have applied a little too much colour to an area of the drawing, you can always remove a certain amount of that by touching your mounting putty to the area and then lifting it away. If you keep the putty warm in your hand for a moment or two it will become 'sticky' and will successfully remove some of the colour.

Using the **Medium Flesh** pencil I have applied a (medium pressure) layer of colour to the bare skin of the nose. I have added a little **White** to the top edge and the lower central line, which serves to indicate the curvature of the nose, by creating highlights.

Next I applied small areas and spots of **Black** around the nose and also used a heavy pressure application of this colour to darken the nostril opening.

Moving on to the lower muzzle I have applied **White** and **Black** to the relevant parts of this area of the face, using a medium pressure to gradually build up the depth of colour and to create the varying shapes. The gentle curves that can be seen in the lines of spots are useful in helping to create a sense of shape and form, so take care to get these right. By taking your time and building these marks slowly, you can more easily adjust their placement if you need to as you draw

As in previous sections of this drawing, take care to make sure that your application lines are following the fur growth.

This is also really important where I have built up the white tone on the chin, because the irregular edge of the fur, highlighted against the grey background, must show the correct angle of fur growth.

In this section I have turned my attention to the ears and the fur over the nape of the tiger's neck.

Using the **White** pencil I have added numerous thin, 'whispy' hairs, around the nearest ear and introduced small areas of **Apricot** along the bottom edge. A heavy application of **Black** to the recess of the ear helps to create a feeling of depth and to make the white hairs stand out. I have also applied more **Black** to the upper edge of the ear and to the stripes behind the ear.

Immediately behind the nearest ear, where the fur is in shadow I have applied a light layer of **Venetian Red**. On the back of the furthest ear I have used the same colour to darken the area beneath the white patch.

Using the **White** pencil I have also begun to create some texture on the fur over the nape of the neck, using short, medium pressure lines. By leaving areas of **Sandstone** showing I have started creating an impression of texture.

One advantage of using Pastelmat is that the texture allows you to apply a pale colour over a dark one. With any paper that has a smooth surface, you can very quickly 'flatten' any texture that exists as you add heavy applications of colour. However the robust surface of Pastelmat remains textured for longer, meaning that it can continue to take more colour.

In this section I have started to build texture in the longer fur areas.

Where I had previously started to create texture over the neck I have now introduced some areas of dark shadows within the fur, using a light application of **Black**. I have extended these shapes and lines further down the neck and by also adding more **White** as well, I have created highlights to help with the impression of texture.

Where the longer fur runs along the jawline of the tiger, I have added longer (and more wavy) lines to indicate the change of fur length. Some of the base grey paper colour is still evident between these lines, which helps to suggest shadows within the fur.

Using a sharp **Black** pencil once more, I have also added more detail to the remaining black stripes. Be careful not to make these black stripes too regular in shape and size. By 'breaking' the dark areas with the occasional white hair tuft, you create a more realistic effect.

Remember (as before) to make sure that any lines that you introduce 'flow' in the direction that the fur grows.

 In this penultimate section I have extended the **White** fur lines down the side of the head and onto the tiger's chest. I have added more texture to the orange fur using **White** (medium pressure). And added some shadows with a light pressure application of Vandyke Brown

The **Black** stripes in this lower part of the drawing have also been built up with more 'heavy pressure' applications of pigment. You can see that I have curved these short black lines to help to indicate the shape of the animal's body.

This section of the drawing that shows the white fur areas of the muzzle, chin and throat, highlights one potential problem that occurs when depicting white animals. If we had drawn this tiger on a white paper, rather than grey, these areas which are white would have been difficult to emphasize. It would then have been important to introduce some background detail or colour, that would allow the white edges and the form of the animal to be clearly delineated, without the need for a 'flattening' outline.

This final stage is all about small refinements and adjustments.

I have used a sharp **Black** pencil and heavy pressure to work along all the stripes to create fine feathered edges that show some of the individual hairs. On the chin I have added a few more **Black** spots.

Using a light pressure with the **Vandyke Brown** and **Venetian Red** I have darkened the shadows on the shoulder. I have also used the same combination to soften the edge of the dark area on the side of the muzzle, which had looked a little too sharp, giving it a 'square' appearance. By softening this edge, I was able to create a more subtle, curved shape to this part of the tiger's face.

Last, but not least, I have added the whiskers using **White** and heavy pressure. It is important to use a sharp pencil, to give a clean line that is applied with one stroke. To ensure that these whiskers are fine enough, you should not be tempted to redraw any of these lines which don't appear quite right, so it is always worth trying a few practice whiskers on a spare piece of paper first.

Whenever I have finished a drawing, whether it has been produced in coloured pencil or graphite, I always apply several light layers of a colourless fixative to the picture to prevent smudging.

There are a number of quality fixatives available from art shops/suppliers, but the one that I use regularly is Daler Rowney's 'Perfix'. (see right).

Some people use hairspray as a cheap option, but these products are not designed with long term endurance and will often 'yellow' with time.

So, if you want your drawing to last (especially if you plan to sell it), then this small financial outlay will be money well spent.

Bengal Tiger (Panthera tigris tigris)

Height (at shoulders): 90 - 110cm

Head/body length: 1.85 - 2.1m

Tail length: 85 -110cm

Body Mass (average): Male 220Kg   Female 140Kg

The Bengal tiger (as it's name suggests) is a member of the Panthera tigris tigris population that frequents the Indian subcontinent.

As they inhabit tropical and sub-tropical regions they tend to have shorter body fur, but can still exhibit some marked variations between individuals.

These variations are seen at their most extreme in the 'white tigers' (see left).

These animals lack the red and yellow pheomelanin pigments that are needed to give the animal it's brown or orange colouration. The eyes, nose and lips remain the normal colour, unlike in an albino animal, which would show no pigmentation at all.

Step by step drawing using graphite pencils.

Materials: (See Materials section pages 8—15)

Surface: Bristol Board 250 gsm

Pencils:

Other papers: Cartridge paper (if you using the grid method), Tracedown or Tracing paper, depending on your preferred transfer method.

Acetate grid: If using the grid method to create your initial drawing

Mounting Putty.

Koh-I-Noor Hardtmuth eraser.

Stump.

Large wash brush.

White gel pen.

Taking the time to draw and trace all the stripes from your reference photo will ensure that you place them in the correct locations and accurately recreate their shape and size. The curve of many of these stripes is crucial to helping you convey the form of the tiger's body.

By using graphite Tracedown, or tracing paper with soft graphite (6B or softer) on the reverse side you will produce a clear outline to work with. This outline can be easily worked over as you draw, or lifted away using your Mounting Putty.

Scan this code to watch a time-lapse video of the complete drawing.

To begin this drawing you can either trace the outline shown right, or create your own outline using the grid method shown on pages 24 & 25. If you use the grid method and you want to increase the size, don't forget to create your second grid with larger squares. If you have traced the image directly you can place this into a photocopier to create a larger version. Once you have prepared your outline you are ready to transfer it.

In this first stage I have begun to add some of the dark stripes and the black areas around the eyes using the **4B** pencil and medium pressure.

Although I am not too concerned with the 'finish' at this point, I have made sure that the pencil lines that have begun to establish the fur detail follow the correct direction of growth (see diagram on page 28).

Working on the upper section I started by adding detail to the ears. I used a graphite coated stump to apply (using an even circular motion), an overall tone to both ears, before using the **Hardtmuth eraser** to 'draw' the pale hairs, by removing fine lines of graphite.

Then, using the **6B** pencil and firm pressure, I have created the dark central section and darkened some of the lines in between the pale hair. Using the same pencil (heavy pressure) I have also begun to add a greater depth of tone to the stripes

Around the black stripes on the crown of the tiger's head I have begun to draw and then blend some short lines with a **B** pencil (medium pressure), to create the orange fur.

In this picture you can see that I have moved down the face adding more orange fur tone using the same techniques as in the previous stage, but making sure to leave the white fur sections above the eyes, untouched.

To begin the eyes, I have used the same stump that I am using for the fur, to apply a soft mid tone over the eye, leaving just a small area of white highlight.

Just as when working with coloured pencil, if you feel at any point that you have applied too much graphite to the drawing, you can easily remove some by gently touching your mounting putty to the drawing and lifting it away. This technique is also useful if you need to create highlights on a particular area of your subject.

Moving down the face to the bridge of the nose, I began (as before) using and blending the **B** pencil, but I have also added shadow to the cleft of the facial centre line and to the right side of the face using the **4B** pencil with medium pressure.

Using the same **4B** pencil I have darkened the iris and created a shadow across the top of each eye, leaving the curved highlights as in the previous stage.

Once again, using the **6B** pencil and heavy pressure I have darkened more of the black stripes.

Whenever you use your stump to blend an area of the drawing, it will lift away a small amount of the graphite. Later in the drawing process, if you need to create an even mid-tone in one part of the drawing, you can rub this graphite coated stump on that 'clean' area and it will quickly and easily create the effect you are looking for.

The focus of this stage is on the fur of the neck and shoulder and also on the right side of the head.

Using medium pressure with the **B** pencil once more for the 'orange' fur, I began by paying close attention to the detail in my reference photo, as this area of fur is complex.

For the upper section of fur I have used a similar technique to the fur of the face, by applying and blending the lines of graphite. However, moving down the neck the fur becomes quite 'clumped' and textured. To achieve this texture I first applied a more even tone with my stump and then worked an irregular pattern of a darker tone over the top, using a tight circular motion with the pencil.

Working further down towards the shoulder I have returned to using the previous adding & blending technique once more.

I have also drawn some more of the black stripes with heavy pressure and the **6B** pencil, making sure that the lines I apply run in the same direction as the detail in the orange fur. Keeping the pencil very sharp enabled me to create the fine, irregular edges which help to suggest the longer nature of this area of fur.

On the right side of the tiger's head I have used a **2H** pencil (medium pressure) to delineate longer fur.

Following on from the previous stage I have continued adding more fur detail onto the shoulder. Where I have added the mid-tone fur, I have also applied some more textural detail with the **B** pencil to indicate the longer fur.

Extending the black stripes further down I have made sure that the pencil lines curve downward to show the change in the direction of fur growth.

On the muzzle I have applied more tone and texture, using the **Stump**, continuing this process down to the nose.

It is a good idea to have a number of stumps available to use. There may be times when you need to blend some detail without adding extra tone, so having a clean one at your disposal is important.

If you need to 'clean' one at any point, you can remove the impregnated layers by rubbing it with a piece of sandpaper. The shape would suggest that they might fit into a pencil sharpener, but unfortunately the blades will not successfully cut through the many layers of paper.

Using the **4B** pencil (medium pressure) I have increased the depth of tone over the top of the muzzle and also down the right hand side, just in front of the eye.

For the nose I used the stump to apply the base tone and then added some spots and shading with the **4B** pencil and then the dark nasal openings were created with heavy pressure of the **6B** pencil.

Using the same **6B** pencil (heavy pressure) I then began the process of adding the numerous lines of spots around the nose and mouth. The curves of these lines are very important in creating a believable 'shape' to the muzzle.

Using heavy pressure and the **6B** pencil once again I have applied longer strokes to show the irregular stripes on the tiger's cheek and jaw.

On the tongue (as with the nose), I used the stump to apply the first layer of graphite and then gradually darkened this area with light pressure using the **4B** pencil.

I have drawn the dark areas of the lips and gums with the **6B** pencil (heavy pressure), taking care to leave some areas of highlights, to show the moist, shiny nature of this area of the face.

On the fur of the chin I have used the **4B** pencil (medium pressure) to show some of the irregular spots, whilst the soft, pale fur was drawn in with a **2H** pencil (light pressure).

In this penultimate section I have added more detail to the longer fur of the shoulder and chest.

The black stripes in this area are broken and irregular, so I have drawn long, curving lines with the **6B** pencil (medium pressure).

The soft, shadow areas of the white chest fur were created using the **Stump** to 'draw' in the fur detail.

In the final picture on the next page I have worked over all the black stripes once more with a sharp **6B** pencil (heavy pressure), to increase the level of detail along their edges.

The orange fur has been darkened in places using the **Stump**, which I first rubbed on my **6B** pencil to allow it to pick up some more graphite, before applying it to the shadow areas of the face and neck.

To finish, I have drawn in the whiskers. On the right side of the face I have added these with fine lines from a sharp **2H** pencil, whereas the whiskers that can be seen clearly as they overlap the tiger's mouth and jaw, have been drawn with single, clean strokes using a **White Gel Pen**.

Completed Bengal Tiger drawing.

About the Artist

Birdwatching on a tributary of the Fraser river in Canada.

Andrew is a self-taught wildlife artist and he works in a variety of media, including graphite pencil, coloured pencil, acrylics and pastel to complete his originals.

Living and working in Oxfordshire, England, he is a keen naturalist and has travelled in both the UK and abroad in search of wildlife.

His artwork has also travelled widely, with examples of his art in collections in the UK, Europe, Kenya, Canada, USA and Nepal.

For the last twenty years he has run numerous workshops and courses in drawing/painting wildlife and has three further books published where he explains his painting and drawing techniques.

His wildlife art has been displayed at many British venues including:

The Mall Galleries   (London)

Nature in Art (Gloucester)

Christies (London)

Sotheby's (Sussex)

The Artist and Illustrator's Show (London),

Art Materials Live (NEC Birmingham)

WWT galleries at Slimbridge, Arundel and The London Wetland Centre.

Index

Printed in Great Britain
by Amazon